A CORNER OF A FOREIGN FIELD

The Illustrated Poetry of the First World War

Selected by Fiona Waters

Photographs from the *Daily Mail*

ATLANTIC WORLD

Atlantic Publishing
38 Copthorne Road
Croxley Green
Hertfordshire, WD3 4AQ, UK

A catalogue record for this book is available from the
British Library.

ISBN: 978-1-909242-05-0

Printed and bound in the UK

FIONA WATERS is 'one of the best anthologists
there are' (*School Librarian*) with the 'born
anthologist's instinct for putting the right poem
in the right place.' (John Mole, *TES*) She has
published more than 70 books including a
number of very successful anthologies. After
many years' experience as a bookseller at
Heffers in Cambridge, Fiona Waters acted
as a consultant on a number of radio and
television book programmes. She is now a
Director of Troubadour and is well known in
the book world for her unparalleled knowledge
of children's books and poetry. She lives in a
17th-century cottage in Dorset with thousands
of books and assorted cats.

CONTENTS

INTRODUCTION

'Are changed, changed utterly:
A terrible beauty is born.'

Those lines are from the poem Easter 1916 by W. B.
Yeats written on 25 September 1916. He was, of course,
writing about another conflict entirely although one
contemporaneous to the First World War. But the words
are curiously apposite since some of the most beautiful
poetry ever written has come from the horror of the
trenches. There are poems dashed off in the full awfulness
of the battlefield; there are others honed with the benefit
of terrible hindsight, certainly not emotion recollected
in tranquillity. And there are poems from an earlier age
which have become inextricably linked to the First World
War because their theme and almost aching beauty exactly
matched the mood of the nation as an entire generation
was lost to the trenches.

'The saviours come not home tonight,
Themselves they could not save.'

Those lines come from the very first poem in the series
of sixty-three poems known as 'A Shropshire Lad' by

A. E. Housman first published privately by the poet in
1896. There are two poems from 'A Shropshire Lad'
in this collection 'On Your Midnight Pallet Lying' and
'Is My Team Ploughing?' These are poems of an earlier
bucolic way of life which are full of despair, despair at
facing death, despair at lost or unrequited love or indeed
forbidden love.

The focus of collections of poems inspired by the
appalling carnage of the years 1914 to 1919 has tended
to be on the mud and blood and terror of the Front and
understandably so, because there is an extraordinarily
deep well to draw from but inevitably these were mostly
written by men. I wanted also to look at those left behind,
the women. The countless mothers, wives, sweethearts,
sisters and daughters whose daily lives were full of the war
and the privations of the war, and yet empty of the grim
experiences of their men folk, unless they were serving
themselves as nurses behind the lines. Life was grim at
home too but not in the same desperately random way as
at the Front. And always there would be the fear of the

unknown. With no easy communication such as we take totally for granted today, months would go by before a precious letter would arrive and, agonisingly, letters would still be arriving after the fateful telegram advising of 'death in action'.

Women took up many of the roles formerly performed by men and this changed most of their lives irrevocably as they found, of necessity, new freedoms and new responsibilities. But these were also the women who mourned the passing of their menfolk not only for the first few frozen months, but for the rest of their lives as there were not many who returned from the Front to the comforts of A. E. Housman's survivor.

> 'Yes, lad, I lie easy,
> I lie as lads would choose:
> I cheer a deadman's sweetheart,
> Never ask me whose.'

Not many of the poems written by women that I have found are in the same poetic league as the better known writings from their male contemporaries but they have a gentle pathos that demands more than a cursory glance. Written by an Australian poet, Nina Murdoch, the third line of the following stanza stabs at the heartstrings.

> 'This is the bitterest wrong the world wide,
> That young men on the battlefield should rot,
> And I be widowed who was scarce a bride,
> While prattling old men sit at ease and plot.'

But to return to W. B. Yeats. The word he uses is beauty, and there is beauty in these poems too. The short but very lovely poem by Isaac Rosenberg 'Returning, We

Hear Larks' alludes to the curious truth that even in adversity there can be delight.

> But hark! joy – joy – strange joy.
> Lo! heights of night ringing with unseen larks.
> Music showering on our upturned list'ning faces.
> Death could drop from the dark
> As easily as song –
> But song only dropped,'

And if you look at so many of the photographic images in this book what you see is relentlessly cheerful faces, smiling in the face of the darkest of adversity. You see comradeship of the most truthful kind. I have included some Soldiers' songs in the collection for the same reason; their devil-may care optimism, making a joke of inedible food, rat infested trenches, incompetent leadership and unspeakable fears and privations. Many of the images in this collection are reproduced for the first time. Taken from the *Daily Mail* archives, those I have chosen capture many of the small moments of un-named individual people in this cataclysmic catastrophe that was branded 'the war to end all wars'.

The poems may well be an 'Anthem for Doomed Youth' but war had never been like this before. Poets have written about war since the dawn of time and continue to do so, yet the stature of the greatest of the World War I poets is unquestioned. Theirs is some of the greatest poetry ever written.

Fiona Waters
Dorset
July 2007

IN FLANDERS FIELDS

ABOVE: *A cap and rifle mark the grave of an unknown soldier*

BELOW: *Rain filling the shell holes created a treacherous terrain*

OPPOSITE ABOVE: *Allied troops on the march*

OPPOSITE BELOW: *Highlanders accompanied by pipers, 31 July 1916*

In Flanders fields the poppies blow
Between the crosses, row on row
That mark our place; and in the sky
The larks, still bravely singing, fly
Scarce heard amid the guns below.

We are the Dead. Short days ago
We lived, felt dawn, saw sunset glow,
Loved and were loved, and now we lie
In Flanders fields.

Take up our quarrel with the foe:
To you from failing hands we throw
The torch; be yours to hold it high.
If ye break faith with us who die
We shall not sleep, though poppies grow
In Flanders fields.

John McCrae

THE CALL

Who's for the trench –
Are you, my laddie?
Who'll follow French –
Will you, my laddie?
Who's fretting to begin,
Who's going out to win?
And who wants to save his skin
Do you, my laddie?

Who's for the khaki suit –
Are you, my laddie?
Who longs to charge and shoot –
Do you, my laddie?
Who's keen on getting fit,
Who means to show his grit,
And who'd rather wait a bit –
Would you, my laddie?

Who'll earn the Empire's thanks –
Will you, my laddie?
Who'll swell the victor's ranks –
Will you, my laddie?
When that procession comes,
Banners and rolling drums –
Who'll stand and bite his thumbs –
Will you, my laddie?

Jessie Pope

BREAKFAST

We ate our breakfast lying on our backs,
Because the shells were screeching overhead.
I bet a rasher to a loaf of bread
That Hull United would beat Halifax
When Jimmy Stainthorp played full-back instead
Of Billy Bradford. Ginger raised his head
And cursed, and took the bet; and dropt back dead.
We ate our breakfast lying on our backs,
Because the shells were screeching overhead.

Wilfrid Gibson

ABOVE: *A meal and rest break for the Leicesters*

IN TRAINING

The wind is cold and heavy
And storms are in the sky:
Our path across the heather
Goes higher and more high.

To right, the town we came from,
To left, blue hills and sea:
The wind is growing colder
And shivering are we.

We drag with stiffening fingers
Our rifles up the hill.
The path is steep and tangled
But leads to Flanders still.

Edward Shanks

ABOVE RIGHT: *Black Watch pipers play to the troops
after the successful capture of Longueval, 14 July 1916*

RIGHT: *'Kitchener's Army'*

'NOW THAT YOU TOO MUST SHORTLY GO THE WAY'

Now that you too must shortly go the way
Which in these bloodshot years uncounted men
Have gone in vanishing armies day by day,
And in their numbers will not come again:
I must not strain the moments of our meeting
Striving each look, each accent, not to miss,
Or question of our parting and our greeting,
Is this the last of all? is this – or this?

Last sight of all it may be with these eyes,
Last touch, last hearing, since eyes, hands, and ears,
Even serving love, are our mortalities,
And cling to what they own in mortal fears: –
But oh, let end what will, I hold you fast
By immortal love, which has no first or last.

Eleanor Farjeon

BELOW: *Christmas in 1916 was celebrated in a shell crater alongside a comrade's grave*

THE SEND-OFF

Down the close, darkening lanes they sang their way
To the siding-shed,
And lined the train with faces grimly gay.

Their breasts were stuck all white with wreath and spray
As men's are, dead.

Dull porters watched them, and a casual tramp
Stood staring hard,
Sorry to miss them from the upland camp.

Then, unmoved, signals nodded, and a lamp
Winked to the guard.

So secretly, like wrongs hushed-up, they went.
They were not ours:
We never heard to which front these were sent.

Nor there if they yet mock what women meant
Who gave them flowers.

Shall they return to beatings of great bells
In wild train-loads?
A few, a few, too few for drums and yells,

May creep back, silent, to still village wells,
Up half-known roads.

TOP: *Refreshments for the wounded*

ABOVE: *Canadians after a successful attack on Vimy Ridge*

BELOW: *A field dressing station after the Battle of Messines, 7 June 1917*

OPPOSITE: *A platoon of the Worcester Regiment march to the western front*

Wilfred Owen

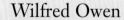

YOUTH IN ARMS I

Happy boy, happy boy,
David the immortal-willed,
Youth a thousand thousand times
Slain, but not once killed,
Swaggering again to-day
In the old contemptuous way;

Leaning backward from your thigh
Up against the tinselled bar –
Dust and ashes! is it you?
Laughing, boasting, there you are!
First we hardly recognised you
In your modern avatar.

Soldier, rifle, brown khaki –
Is your blood as happy so?
Where's your sling, or painted shield,
Helmet, pike, or bow?
Well, you're going to the wars –
That is all you need to know.

Greybeards plotted. They were sad.
Death was in their wrinkled eyes.
At their tables, with their maps
Plans and calculations, wise
They all seemed; for well they knew
How ungrudgingly Youth dies.

At their green official baize
They debated all the night
Plans for your adventurous days,
Which you followed with delight,
Youth in all your wanderings,
David of a thousand slings.

Harold Monro

A KISS

She kissed me when she said good-bye –
A child's kiss, neither bold nor shy.

We had met but a few short summer hours;
Talked of the sun, the wind, the flowers,

Sports and people; had rambled through
A casual catchy song or two,

And walked with arms linked to the car
By the light of a single misty star.

(It was war-time, you see, and the streets were dark
Lest the ravishing Hun should find a mark.)

And so we turned to say good-bye;
But somehow or other, I don't know why,

– Perhaps 'twas the feel of the khaki coat
(She'd a brother in Flanders then) that smote

Her heart with a sudden tenderness
Which issued in that swift caress –

Somehow, to her, at any rate
A mere hand-clasp seemed inadequate;

And so she lifted her dewy face
And kissed me – but without a trace

Of passion, – and we said good-bye …
A child's kiss, … neither bold nor shy.

My friend, I like you – it seemed to say –
Here's to our meeting again some day!
Some happier day …
Good-bye.

Bernard Freeman Trotter

WARBRIDE

There has been wrong done since the world began,
That young men should go out and die in war,
And lie face down in the dust for a brief span,
And be not good to look at any more.

It is the old men with their crafty eyes
And greedy fingers and their feeble lungs,
Make mischief in the world and are called wise,
And bring war on us with their garrulous tongues.

It is the old men hid in secret rooms,
Feign wisdom while they sign our peace away,
And turn fair meadows into reeking tombs,
And passionate bridegrooms into bloodied clay.

It is the old men should be sent to fight!
The old men grown so wise they have forgot
The touch of mouth on mouth in the still night,
The tenderness that wedded lovers wot;

The dreams that dwell in the eyes of a young bride;
The secret beauty of things said and done;
The hope of children coming, and the pride
Of little homes and gardens in the sun.

It is the old men that have nought to lose,
And nought to pray for but their gasping breath,
Should bear this ill of the world, and so choose
Out of their beds to meet their master, Death.

This is the bitterest wrong the world wide,
That young men on the battlefield should rot,
And I be widowed who was scarce a bride,
While prattling old men sit at ease and plot.

Nina Murdoch

OPPOSITE LEFT: *'Tommy' celebrates Christmas*

OPPOSITE RIGHT: *Families prepare for the inevitable separation as soldiers return to the front*

ABOVE: *One of the many women relied upon to keep the railways running*

BELOW: *Nurses seek cover at the Fifth Canadian Hospital*

TELLING THE BEES

They dug no grave for our soldier lad, who fought and who died out there:

Bugle and drum for him were dumb, and the padre said no prayer;

The passing bell gave never a peal to warn that a soul was fled,

And we laid him not in the quiet spot where cluster his kin that are dead.

But I hear a foot on the pathway, above the low hum of the hive,

That at edge of dark, with the song of the lark, tells that the world is
    alive:

The master starts on his errand, his tread is heavy and slow,

Yet he cannot choose but tell the news – the bees have a right to know.

Bound by the ties of a happier day, they are one with us now in our worst;

On the very morn that my boy was born they were told the tidings the first:

With what pride they will hear of the end he made, and the ordeal that he
    trod

Of the scream of shell, and the venom of hell, and the flame of the sword of
    God.

Wise little heralds, tell of my boy, in your golden tabard coats.

Tell the bank where he slept, and the stream he leapt, where the spangled
    lily floats;

The tree he climbed shall lift her head, and the torrent he swam shall
    thrill,

And the tempest that bore his shouts before shall cry his message still.

G. E. R.

BELOW LEFT: *Noyon 1917: Women, children and the old queue for basic provisions*

BELOW RIGHT: *A British intelligence sergeant examines a civilian's papers*

TO MY BROTHER

(In Memory of July 1st 1916)

Your battle-wounds are scars upon my heart,
Received when in that grand and tragic 'show'
You played your part
Two years ago,

And silver in the summer morning sun
I see the symbol of your courage glow –
That Cross you won
Two years ago.

Though now again you watch the shrapnel fly,
And hear the guns that daily louder grow,
As in July
Two years ago,

May you endure to lead the Last Advance
And with your men pursue the flying foe
As once in France
Two years ago.

ABOVE: *Household goods provide an effective barrier in Bailleul*

BELOW: *1915: Troops face a second winter*

Vera Brittain

SOCKS

Shining pins that dart and click
In the fireside's sheltered peace
Check the thoughts that cluster thick –
20 plain and then decrease.

He was brave – well, so was I –
Keen and merry, but his lip
Quivered when he said good-bye –
Purl the seam-stitch, purl and slip.

Never used to living rough,
Lots of things he'd got to learn;
Wonder if he's warm enough –
Knit 2, catch 2, knit 1, turn.

Hark! The paper-boys again!
Wish that shout could be suppressed;
Keeps one always on the strain –
Knit off 9, and slip the rest.

Wonder if he's fighting now,
What he's done and where he's been;
He'll come out on top, somehow –
Slip 1, knit 2, purl 14.

Jessie Pope

ABOVE: *The flooded trenches often led to trenchfoot*

BELOW LEFT: *Under cover in the trenches, using a camouflaged periscope to keep watch*

BELOW RIGHT: *Troops on the eastern front wrap up against the cold*

MY SWEET OLD ETCETERA

my sweet old etcetera
aunt lucy during the recent

war could and what
is more did tell you just
what everybody was fighting

for,
my sister

isabel created hundreds
(and
hundreds) of socks not to
mention shirts fleaproof earwarmers

etcetera wristers etcetera, my
mother hoped that

i would die etcetera
bravely of course my father used
to become hoarse talking about how it was
a privilege and if only he
could meanwhile my

self etcetera lay quictly
in the deep mud et

cetera
(dreaming,
et
    cetera, of
Your smile
eyes knees and of your Etcetera)

e. e. cummings

BELOW: *A soldier wades into the waterlogged trenches*

BREAK OF DAY IN THE TRENCHES

The darkness crumbles away.
It is the same old druid Time as ever.
Only a live thing leaps my hand,
A queer sardonic rat,
As I pull the parapet's poppy
To stick behind my ear.
Droll rat, they would shoot you if they knew
Your cosmopolitan sympathies.
Now you have touched this English hand
You will do the same to a German
Soon, no doubt, if it be your pleasure
To cross the sleeping green between.
It seems you inwardly grin as you pass
Strong eyes, fine limbs, haughty athletes,

Less chanced than you for life,
Bonds to the whims of murder,
Sprawled in the bowels of the earth,
The torn fields of France.
What do you see in our eyes
At the shrieking iron and flame
Hurled through still heavens?
What quaver – what heart aghast?
Poppies whose roots are in man's veins
Drop, and are ever dropping;
But mine in my ear is safe,
Just a little white with the dust.

Isaac Rosenberg

BELOW: *Devastation after battle*

ATTACK

At dawn the ridge emerges massed and dun
In wild purple of the glow'ring sun,
Smouldering through spouts of drifting smoke that shroud
The menacing scarred slope; and, one by one,
Tanks creep and topple forward to the wire.
The barrage roars and lifts. Then, clumsily bowed
With bombs and guns and shovels and battle-gear,
Men jostle and climb to meet the bristling fire.
Lines of grey, muttering faces, masked with fear,
They leave their trenches, going over the top,
While time ticks blank and busy on their wrists,
And hope, with furtive eyes and grappling fists,
Flounders in mud. O Jesus, make it stop!

Siegfried Sassoon

ABOVE: *Soldiers launch an attack*

BELOW: *Respirators were developed to counter the threat of poisoned gas attacks*

'THEY'

The Bishop tells us: 'When the boys come back
They will not be the same; for they'll have fought
In a just cause: they lead the last attack
On Anti-Christ; their comrades' blood has bought
New right to breed an honourable race,
They have challenged Death and dared him face to face.'

'We're none of us the same!' the boys reply.
'For George lost both his legs; and Bill's stone blind;
Poor Jim's shot through the lungs and like to die;
And Bert's gone syphilitic: you'll not find
A chap who's served that hasn't found *some* change.'
And the Bishop said: 'The ways of God are strange!'

Siegfried Sassoon

ABOVE: *Members of the 11th East Lancashire Regiment, known as the 'Accrington Pals'*

RIGHT: *Soldiers mock up an old hansom cab as a 'seat of power'*

BILLET

O, but the racked clear tired strained frames we had!

Tumbling in the new billet on to straw bed,

Dead asleep in eye shutting. Waking as sudden

To a golden and azure roof, a golden ratcheted

Lovely web of blue seen and blue shut, and cobwebs and tiles,

And grey wood dusty with time. June's girlish kindest smiles.

Rest at last and no danger for another week, a seven-day week.

But one Private took on himself a Company's heart to speak,

'I wish to bloody hell I was just going to Brewery – surely

To work all day (in Stroud) and be free at tea-time – allowed

Resting when one wanted, and a joke in season,

To change clothes and take a girl to Horsepool's turning,

Or drink a pint at 'Travellers Rest', and find no cloud.

Then God and man and war and Gloucestershire would have
   a reason,

But I get no good in France, getting killed, cleaning off mud.

He spoke the heart of all of us – the hidden thought burning,
   unturning.

Ivor Gurney

LEFT: *A shelter and a brazier to help troops keep warm and dry*

BELOW: *Nissen hut camp*

'WHEN THIS BLOODY WAR IS OVER'

When this bloody war is over,
No more soldiering for me.
When I get my civvy clothes on,
Oh, how happy I shall be!
No more church parades on Sunday,
No more begging for a pass.
You can tell the Sergeant-Major
To stick his passes up his arse.

When this bloody war is over,
No more soldiering for me.
When I get my civvy clothes on,
Oh, how happy I shall be!
No more NCOs to curse me,
No more rotten army stew.
You can tell the old Cook-Sergeant,
To stick his stew right up his flue.

When this bloody war is over,
No more soldiering for me.
When I get my civvy clothes on,
Oh, how happy I shall be!
No more sergeants bawling
'Pick it up' and 'Put it down.'
If I meet the ugly bastard
I'll kick his arse all over town.

Soldiers' song

ABOVE: *Triumphant Allied troops*

BELOW: *Soldiers seek the warmth of a fire, January 1918*

RENDEZVOUS

I have a rendezvous with Death
At some disputed barricade,
When Spring comes back with rustling shade
And apple-blossoms fill the air –
I have a rendezvous with Death
When Spring brings back blue days and fair.

It may be he shall take my hand
And lead me into his dark land
And close my eyes and quench my breath –
It may be I shall pass him still.
I have a rendezvous with Death
On some scarred slope of battered hill,
When Spring comes round again this year
And the first meadow-flowers appear.

God knows 'twere better to be deep
Pillowed in silk and scented down,
Where love throbs out in blissful sleep,
Pulse nigh to pulse, and breath to breath,
Where hushed awakenings are dear …
But I've a rendezvous with Death
At midnight in some flaming town,
When Spring trips north again this year,
And I to my pledged word am true,
I shall not fail that rendezvous.

Alan Seeger

ABOVE: *Troops at the end of the four-and-a-half-month Somme offensive*

RIGHT: *Allied troops sheltering in a German observation post at Messines Ridge*

AN IRISH AIRMAN
FORESEES HIS DEATH

I know that I shall meet my fate
Somewhere among the clouds above;
Those that I fight I do not hate,
Those that I guard I do not love;
My country is Kiltartan Cross,
My countrymen Kiltartan's poor,
No likely end could bring them loss
Or leave them happier than before.
Nor law, nor duty bade me fight,
Nor public men, nor cheering crowds,
A lonely impulse of delight
Drove to this tumult in the clouds;
I balanced all, brought all to mind,
The years to come seemed waste of breath,
A waste of breath the years behind
In balance with this life, this death.

W. B. Yeats

BELOW: *An Allied bomb destined for the Rhine*   ABOVE: *Marines march into France*

THE DEATH OF A SOLDIER

Life contracts and death is expected,
As in a season of autumn.
The soldier falls.

He does not become a three-days personage,
Imposing his separation,
Calling for pomp.

Death is absolute and without memorial,
As in a season of autumn,
When the wind stops,

When the wind stops and, over the heavens,
The clouds go, nevertheless,
In their direction.

Wallace Stevens

TOP: *German casualties on the battlefields of Flanders*

ABOVE: *German soldiers killed in action*

27

THE LEVELLER

Near Martinpuich that night of Hell
Two men were struck by the same shell,
Together tumbling in one heap
Senseless and limp like slaughtered sheep.

One was a pale eighteen-year-old,
Blue-eyed and thin and not too bold,
Pressed for the war not ten years too soon,
The shame and pity of his platoon.

The other came from far-off lands
With bristling chin and whiskered hands,
He had known death and hell before
In Mexico and Ecuador.

Yet in his death this cut-throat wild
Groaned 'Mother! Mother!' like a child,
While that poor innocent in man's clothes
Died cursing God with brutal oaths.

Old Sergeant Smith, kindest of men,
Wrote out two copies, there and then
Of his accustomed funeral speech
To cheer the womenfolk of each: –

'He died a hero's death: and we
His Comrades of "A" Company
Deeply regret his death: we shall
All deeply miss so dear a pal.'

Robert Graves

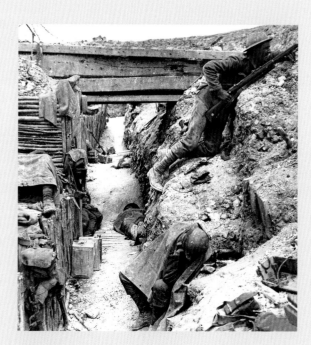

LEFT: *After the battle*

ABOVE: *An Allied soldier keeps watch in a captured German trench*

OPPOSITE: *Channels are dug in an attempt to drain surface water*

RAIN! RAIN! RAIN!

Ever since I landed here,
Things have looked so dull and drear,
Wonder if this war's in vain,
Wonder why there's so much rain?

My face and hands badly peeled,
Playing 'Mock War' in sodden fields,
Body aches from chills and pains,
Still it rains and rains, and rains.

Tomorrow we'll be on our way,
To 'The Front' I heard them say,
Tonight we loaded on the trains,
Wonder why it rains and rains?

The guy who wrote 'bout Sunny France,
Must have been in an awful trance,
Wisht ol' sun would come peepin' thru,
Perhaps I wouldn't feel so blue.

Clouds a-skootin' fast overhead,
Hiked thru mud 'till I'm damn near dead,
Gee! I'm wet clear thru to the skin,
Wonder when we're 'Goin' In'?

Earth seems to be a-quiver with fright,
Gosh, I'd like to be home tonight,
Never thot I'd be 'Over Here',
Lord, this rain makes a fellow feel queer.

Been in the lines near thirty days,
Know I'm changed in lots of ways;
Now I know why I had that trainin',
Wonder if it ever will stop rainin'?

Relieved from the 'lines' last night,
Gee, but this beard of mine's a fright,
Hiked a thousand kilos more,
Damn this rain it's making me sore.

Been soaking wet since September,
Here it is 'way up in November;
But now old Heinie's on the run,
Wonder if this rain's rainin' for fun?

Boys are not talking much today,
What they're thinking none can say,
Just got the news that 'War is done,'
Must be right *'cause there's the ol' sun!*

Rhymes of a Lost Battalion Doughboy

OF GRANDCOURT

Through miles of mud we travelled, and by sick valleys –
The Valley of Death at last – most evil alleys,
To Grandcourt trenches reserve – and the hell's name it did
    deserve.
Rain there was – tired and weak I was, glad for an end.
But one spoke to me – one I liked well as friend –
'Let's volunteer for the Front Line – many others won't.
I'll volunteer, it's better being there than here.'
But I had seen too many ditches and stood too long
Feeling my feet freeze, and my shoulders ache with the
    strong
Pull of equipment – and too much use of pain and strain.
Besides he was Lance Corporal and might be full Corporal
Before the next straw resting might come again,
Before the next billet should hum with talk and song.
Stars looked as well from second as from first line holes.
There were fatigues for change, and a thought less danger –
But five or six there were followed Army with their souls –
Took five days' dripping rain without let or finish again –
With dysentery and bodies of heroic ghouls.
Till at last their hearts feared nothing of the brazen anger,
(Perhaps of death little) but once more again to drop on straw
    bed-serving,
And to have heaven of dry feeling after the damps and fouls.

Ivor Gurney

ABOVE: *A crossing point on the River Somme near Peronne*

BELOW: *January 1918: the mud was ever-present*

EASTER MONDAY

In the last letter that I had from France
You thanked me for the silver Easter egg
Which I had hidden in the box of apples
You liked to munch beyond all other fruit.
You found the egg the Monday before Easter,
And said, 'I will praise Easter Monday now –
It was such a lovely morning.' Then you spoke
Of the coming battle and said, 'This is the eve.
Goodbye. And may I have a letter soon.'

That Easter Monday was a day for praise,
It was such a lovely morning. In our garden
We sowed our earliest seeds, and in the orchard
The apple-bud was ripe. It was the eve.
There are three letters that you will not get.

Eleanor Farjeon

ABOVE LEFT: *A postal delivery from Blighty*

LEFT: *Sorting mail from home, 1915*

SING A SONG OF WAR-TIME

Sing a song of War-time,
Soldiers marching by,
Crowds of people standing,
Waving them 'Good-bye'.
When the crowds are over,
Home we go to tea,
Bread and margarine to eat,
War economy!

If I ask for cake, or
Jam of any sort,
Nurse says, 'What! In War-time?
Archie, cert'nly not!'
Life's not very funny
Now, for little boys,
Haven't any money,
Can't buy any toys.

Mummie does the house-work,
Can't get any maid,
Gone to make munitions,
'Cause they're better paid,
Nurse is always busy,
Never time to play,
Sewing shirts for soldiers,
Nearly ev'ry day.

Ev'ry body's doing
Something for the War,
Girls are doing things
They've never done before,
Go as 'bus conductors,
Drive a car or van,
All the world is topsy-turvy
Since the War began.

Nina Macdonald

ABOVE: *'Tar women' expertly mending the roads*

RIGHT: *Female guards employed on the London underground*

CHRISTMAS 1916: THOUGHTS IN A V.A.D.
HOSPITAL KITCHEN

There's no Xmas leave for us scullions,
We've got to keep on with the grind:
Just cooking for Britain's heroes.
But, bless you! we don't really mind.

We've scores and scores of potatoes,
And cabbages also to do;
And onions, and turnips, and what not,
That go in the Irish stew.

We're baking, and frying, and boiling,
From morning until night;
But we've got to keep on a bit longer,
Till Victory comes in sight.

Then there's cutting the thin bread and butter,
For the men who are very ill;
But we feel we're well rewarded;
For they've fought old Kaiser Bill.

Yes! we've got to hold on a while longer,
Till we've beaten the Hun to his knees:
And *then* 'Good-bye' to the kitchen;
The treacle, the jam, and the cheese!

M. Winifred Wedgwood

RIGHT: *Lincolnshire Land Girls*

BELOW: *British prisoners return home*

33

WOMEN AT MUNITION MAKING

Their hands should minister unto the
    flame of life,
Their fingers guide
The rosy teat, swelling with milk,
To the eager mouth of the suckling
    babe
Or smooth with tenderness,
Softly and soothingly,
The heated brow of the ailing child.
Or stray among the curls
Of the boy or girl, thrilling to mother
    love.
But now,
Their hands, their fingers
Are coarsened in munition factories.
Their thoughts, which should fly
Like bees among the sweetest mind
    flowers,
Gaining nourishment for the thoughts
    to be,
Are bruised against the law,
    'Kill, kill'.

They must take part in defacing and
    destroying the natural body
Which, certainly during this
    dispensation
Is the shrine of the spirit.
O God!
Throughout the ages we have seen,
Again and again
Men by Thee created
Cancelling each other.
And we have marvelled at the seeming
    annihilation
Of Thy work.
But this goes further,
Taints the fountain head,
Mounts like a poison to the Creator's
    very heart.
O God!
Must It anew be sacrificed on earth?

Mary Gabrielle Collins

WAR GIRLS

There's the girl who clips your ticket for the train,
And the girl who speeds the lift from floor to floor,
There's the girl who does a milk-round in the rain,
And the girl who calls for orders at your door.
Strong, sensible, and fit,
They're out to show their grit,
And tackle jobs with energy and knack.
No longer caged and penned up,
They're going to keep their end up
Till the khaki soldier boys come marching back.

There's the motor girl who drives a heavy van,
There's the butcher girl who brings your joint of meat,
There's the girl who cries 'All fares, please!' like a man,
And the girl who whistles taxis up the street.
Beneath each uniform
Beats a heart that's soft and warm,
Though of canny mother-wit they show no lack;
But a solemn statement this is,
They've no time for love and kisses
Till the khaki soldier boys come marching back.

Jessie Pope

ABOVE: *The female workforce at a paper mill at Purfleet on the Thames*

BELOW: *A female 'coalie' makes a delivery*

OPPOSITE: *French women making shells*

THE V.A.D. SCULLERY-MAID'S SONG

Washing up the dishes;
Washing up the plates;
Washing up the greasy tins,
That everybody hates.

Scouring out the buckets;
Cleaning down the stoves.
Guess I'm going to 'stick it',
Though my fancy roves.

Washing 'for duration',
That's what I will do;
As I've got no head-piece
For the cooking too.

Others are much smarter;
More clever, too, than I.
Still I go on 'charing';
Singing cheerfully –

'Washing up the dishes;
Washing up the plates;
Washing up the greasy tins,
Which everybody hates.'

M. Winifred Wedgwood

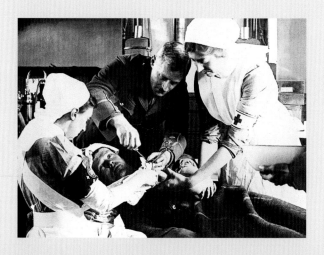

RIGHT: *Voluntary Aid Detachment nurses care for a wounded British soldier*

BELOW: *Nurses practise fire drills in case of enemy attack*

THE ADMONITION: TO BETSEY

Remember, on your knees,
The men who guard your slumbers –

And guard a house in a still street
Of drifting leaves and drifting feet,
A deep blue window where below
Lies moonlight on the roofs like snow,
A clock that still the quarters tells
To the dove that roosts beneath the bell's
Grave canopy of silent brass
Round which the little night winds pass
Yet stir it not in the grey steeple;
And guard all small and drowsy people
Whom gentlest dusk doth disattire,
Undressing by the nursery fire
In unperturbed numbers
On this side of the seas –

Remember, on your knees,
The men who guard your slumbers.

Helen Parry Eden

ABOVE: *Two children set off on their
holiday from Waterloo Station, May 1914*

LEFT: *Canadian infantrymen,
10 October 1916*

37

TRENCH IDYLL

We sat together in the trench,
He on a lump of frozen earth
Blown in the night before,
I on an unexploded shell;
And smoked and talked, like exiles,
Of how pleasant London was,
Its women, restaurants, night clubs, theatres,
How at that very hour
The taxi-cabs were taking folk to dine …
Then we sat silent for a while
As a machine-gun swept the parapet.

He said:
'I've been here on and off two years
And seen only one man killed'.

'That's odd.'

'The bullet hit him in the throat:
He fell in a heap on the fire-step,
And called out "My God! *dead!*"'

'Good Lord, how terrible!'

'Well, as to that, the nastiest job I've had
Was last year on this very front
Taking the discs at night from men
Who'd hung for six months on the wire
Just over there.
The worst of all was
They fell to pieces at a touch.
Thank God we couldn't see their faces;
They had gas helmets on …'

I shivered;
'It's rather cold here, sir, suppose we move?'

Richard Aldington

BELOW LEFT: *Soldiers survey the battlefields*   BELOW RIGHT: *Maintaining the trenches*

WINTER WARFARE

Colonel Cold strode up the Line
(tabs of rime and spurs of ice);
stiffened all that met his glare:
horses, men, and lice.

Visited a forward post,
left them burning, ear to foot;
fingers stuck to biting steel,
toes to frozen boot.

Stalked on into No Man's Land,
turned the wire to fleecy wool,
iron stakes to sugar sticks
snapping at a pull.

Those who watched with hoary eyes
saw two figures gleaming there;
Hauptmann Kalte, Colonel Cold,
gaunt in the grey air.

Stiffly, tinkling spurs they moved,
glassy-eyed, with glinting heel
stabbing those who lingered there
torn by screaming steel.

Edgell Rickword

ABOVE: *Harsh winter conditions in 1916-17*

RIGHT: *Royal Scots Fusiliers in 1914*

REMORSE

Lost in the swamp and welter of the pit,
He flounders off the duck-boards; only he knows
Each flash and spouting crash; – each instant lit
When gloom reveals the streaming rain. He goes
Heavily, blindly on. And, while he blunders,
'Could anything be worse than this?' – he wonders,
Remembering how he saw those Germans run,
Screaming for mercy among the stumps of trees:
Green-faced, they dodged and darted: there was one
Livid with terror, clutching at his knees…
Our chaps were sticking 'em like pigs…
'Oh Hell!' He thought – 'there's things in war one dare
Not tell poor father sitting safe at home, who reads
Of dying heroes and their deathless deeds.'

Siegfried Sassoon

ABOVE: *The East Anglian Regiment on the first day of the Battle of Cambrai*

BELOW: *Soldiers look for a way to release a horse sucked into the mud*

A SON

My son was killed while laughing at some jest. I would
   I knew
What it was, and it might serve me in a time when jests
   are few.

Rudyard Kipling

LEFT: *Highland troops embark on a dawn attack*

THE GENERAL

"Good-morning, good-morning!" the General said
When we met him last week on our way to the line.
Now the soldiers he smiled at are most of 'cm dead.
And we're cursing his staff for incompetent swine.
"He's a cheery old card," grunted Harry to Jack
As they slogged up to Arras with rifle and pack.

But he did for them both by his plan of attack.

Siegfried Sassoon

BELOW: *A senior military strategist surveys the battlefield*   ABOVE: *General Robert Nivelle returns to the battlefield, April 1917*

THE RIDGE: 1919

Here on the ridge where the shrill north-easter trails
Low clouds along the snow,
And in a streaming moonlit vapour veils
The peopled earth below,

Let me, O life, a little while forget
The horror of past years –
Man and his agony and bloody sweat,
The terror and the tears,

And struggle only with the mist and snow
Against the hateless wind,
Till scourged and shriven I again may go
To dwell among my kind.

Wilfrid Gibson

ABOVE: *On the attack during the Dardanelles campaign*

BELOW: *The River Ancre a month after the Somme offensive*

STRANGE HELLS

There are strange hells within the minds war made
Not so often, not so humiliatingly afraid
As one would have expected – the racket and fear guns made.
One hell the Gloucester soldiers they quite put out:
Their first bombardment, when in combined black shout

Of fury, guns aligned, they ducked lower their heads
And sang with diaphragms fixed beyond all dreads,
That tin and stretched-wire tinkle, that blither of tune:
'Après la guerre fini', till hell all had come down,
Twelve-inch, six-inch, and eighteen pounders hammering
    hell's thunders.

ABOVE: *The battlefield at Arras*

BELOW: *A wounded soldier rescued by stretcher bearers, September 1917*

Where are they now, on state-doles, or showing shop-patterns
Or walking town to town sore in borrowed tatterns
Or begged. Some civic routine one never learns.
The heart burns – but has to keep out of face how heart burns.

Ivor Gurney

DULCE ET DECORUM EST

Bent double, like old beggars under sacks,
Knock-kneed, coughing like hags, we cursed through
   sludge,
Till on the haunting flares we turned our backs,
And towards our distant rest began to trudge.
Men marched asleep. Many had lost their boots,
But limped on, blood-shod. All went lame; all blind;
Drunk with fatigue; deaf even to the hoots
Of gas-shells dropping softly behind.

Gas! Gas! Quick, boys! – An ecstasy of fumbling,
Fitting the clumsy helmets just in time,
But someone still was yelling out and stumbling
And floundering like a man in fire or lime ...
Dim, through the misty panes and thick green light,
As under a green sea, I saw him drowning.
In all my dreams, before my helpless sight,
He plunges at me, guttering, choking, drowning.

If in some smothering dreams you too could pace
Behind the wagon that we flung him in,
And watch the white eyes writhing in his face,
His hanging face, like a devil's sick of sin;
If you could hear, at every jolt, the blood
Come gargling from the froth-corrupted lungs,
Obscene as cancer, bitter as the cud
Of vile, incurable sores on innocent tongues, –
My friend, you would not tell with such high zest
To children ardent for some desperate glory,
The old Lie: Dulce et decorum est
Pro patria mori.

Wilfred Owen

RIGHT: *The futile attempt to keep equipment dry
in Flanders, 1917*

BELOW: *The mud-soaked fields of Flanders*

POEM

Abbreviated from the Conversation of Mr T. E. H.

Over the flat slope of St Eloi
A wide wall of sandbags.
Night,
In the silence desultory men
Pottering over small fires, cleaning their mess-tins:
To and fro, from the lines,
Men walk as on Piccadilly,
Making paths in the dark,
Through scattered dead horses,
Over a dead Belgian's belly.

The Germans have rockets. The English have no
    rockets.
Behind the lines, cannon, hidden, lying back miles.
Before the line, chaos:

My mind is a corridor. The minds about me are
    corridors.
Nothing suggests itself. There is nothing to do but keep on.

Ezra Pound

TOP: *Cleaning rifles after the battle*

ABOVE: *Bazentin-le-Petit, July 1916*

A DEAD BOCHE

To you who'd read my songs of War
And only hear of blood and fame,
I'll say (you've heard it said before)
'War's Hell!' and if you doubt the same,
To-day I found in Mametz Wood
A certain cure for lust of blood:

Where, propped against a shattered trunk,
In a great mess of things unclean,
Sat a dead Boche; he scowled and stunk
With clothes and face a sodden green,
Big-bellied, spectacled, crop-haired,
Dribbling black blood from nose and beard.

Robert Graves

TOP: *German casualties, 11 July 1916*

ABOVE: *The dead wait for burial*

THE DUG-OUT

Why do you lie with your legs ungainly huddled,
And one arm bent across your sullen, cold,
Exhausted face? It hurts my heart to watch you,
Deep-shadow'd from the candle's guttering gold;
And you wonder why I shake you by the shoulder;
Drowsy, you mumble and sigh and turn your head…
You are too young to fall asleep for ever;
And when you sleep you remind me of the dead.

Siegfried Sassoon

ABOVE LEFT: *Keeping watch*

LEFT: *Dug-outs used during the Second Battle of Ypres*

TO GERMANY

You are blind like us. Your hurt no man designed,
And no man claimed the conquest of your land.
But gropers both through fields of thought confined
We stumble and we do not understand.
You only saw your future bigly planned,
And we, the tapering paths of our own mind,
And in each other's dearest ways we stand,
And hiss and hate. And the blind fight the blind.

When it is peace, then we may view again
With new-won eyes each other's truer form
And wonder. Grown more loving-kind and warm
We'll grasp firm hands and laugh at the old pain,
When it is peace. But until peace, the storm,
The darkness and the thunder and the rain.

Charles Hamilton Sorley

BELOW: *British troops watch as a German prisoner is escorted away*

GROTESQUE

These are the damned circles Dante trod,

Terrible in hopelessness,

But even skulls have their humour,

An eyeless and sardonic mockery:

And we,

Sitting with streaming eyes in the acrid smoke,

That murks our foul, damp billet,

Chant bitterly, with raucous voices

As a choir of frogs

In hideous irony, our patriotic songs.

Frederic Manning

LEFT: *The battered landscape after Nivelle's spring offensive in 1917*

A PRIVATE

ABOVE: *28 October 1917*

BELOW: *Soldiers rest, March 1918*

This ploughman dead in battle slept out of doors

Many a frozen night, and merrily

Answered staid drinkers, good bedmen, and all bores:

'At Mrs Greenland's Hawthorn Bush', said he,

'I slept'. None knew which bush. Above the town,

Beyond 'The Drover', a hundred spot the down

In Wiltshire. And where now at last he sleeps

More sound in France – that, too, he secret keeps.

Edward Thomas

FIRST TIME IN

After the dread tales and red yarns of the Line
Anything might have come to us; but the divine
Afterglow brought us up to a Welsh colony
Hiding in sandbag ditches, whispering consolatory
Soft foreign things. Then we were taken in
To low huts candle-lit, shaded close by slitten
Oilsheets, and there the boys gave us kind welcome,
So that we looked out as from the edge of home.
Sang us Welsh things, and changed all former notions
To human hopeful things. And the next day's guns
Nor any line-pangs ever quite could blot out
That strangely beautiful entry to war's rout;
Candles they gave us, precious and shared over-rations –
Ulysses found little more in his wanderings without doubt.
'David of the White Rock', the 'Slumber Song' so soft, and that
Beautiful tune to which roguish words by Welsh pit boys
Are sung – but never more beautiful than here under the guns' noise.

TOP: *May 1915*

ABOVE: *Soldiers on their
way to the front*

Ivor Gurney

TRUCE

It begins with one or two soldiers
And one or two following
With hampers over their shoulders.
They might be off wildfowling

As they would another Christmas Day,
So gingerly they pick their steps.
No one seems sure of what to do.
All stop when one stops.

A fire gets lit. Some spread
Their greatcoats on the frozen ground.
Polish vodka, fruit and bread
Are broken out and passed round.

The air of an old German song,
The rules of Patience, are the secrets
They'll share before long.
They draw on their last cigarettes

As Friday-night lovers, when it's over,
Might get up from their mattresses
To congratulate each other
And exchange names and addresses.

Paul Muldoon

RIGHT: *Tommy Aitkins*

BELOW: *A welcome Christmas postbag arrives*

A SHROPSHIRE LAD: XXVII

'Is my team ploughing,
That I was used to drive
And hear the harness jingle
When I was man alive?'

Ay, the horses trample,
The harness jingles now;
No change though you lie under
The land you used to plough.

'Is football playing
Along the river shore,
With lads to chase the leather,
Now I stand up no more?'

Ay, the ball is flying,
The lads play heart and soul;
The goal stands up, the keeper
Stands up to keep the goal.

'Is my girl happy,
That I thought hard to leave,
And has she tired of weeping
As she lies down at eve?'

Ay, she lies down lightly,
She lies not down to weep:
Your girl is well contented.
Be still, my lad, and sleep.

'Is my friend hearty,
Now I am thin and pine,
And has he found to sleep in
A better bed than mine?'

Yes, lad, I lie easy,
I lie as lads would choose;
I cheer a dead man's sweetheart,
Never ask me whose.

A. E. Housman

ABOVE: *Railside cemetery on the western front*

BELOW: *Pilckem, August 1917*

THE DEAD FOX HUNTER

In Memory Of Captain A. L. Samson, 2nd Batallion Royal Welch Fusiliers, Killed Near Cuinchy, Sept 15th 1915

We found the little captain at the head;
His men lay well aligned.
We touched his hand – stone cold – and he was dead,
And they, all dead behind,
Had never reached their goal, but they died well;
They charged in line, and in the same line fell.

The well-known rosy colours of his face
Were almost lost in grey.
We saw that, dying and in hopeless case,
For others' sake that day
He'd smothered all rebellious groans: in death
His fingers were tight clenched between his teeth.

For those who live uprightly and die true
Heaven has no bars or locks,
And serves all taste … or what's for him to do
Up there, but hunt the fox?

Angelic choirs? No, Justice must provide
For one who rode straight and in hunting died.

So if Heaven had no Hunt before he came,
Why, it must find one now:
If any shirk and doubt they know the game,
There's one to teach them how:
And the whole host of Seraphim complete
Must jog in scarlet to his opening Meet.

Robert Graves

RIGHT: *A soldier dives for cover*

BELOW: *Casualties from the Third Battle of Ypres*

SOLDIERS

Brother,
I saw you on a muddy road
in France
pass by with your battalion,
rifle at the slope, full marching order,
arm swinging;
and I stood at ease,
folding my hands over my rifle,
with my battalion.
You passed me by, and our eyes met.
We had not seen each other since the days
we climbed the Devon hills together:
our eyes met, startled;
and, because the order was Silence,
we dared not speak.

O face of my friend,
alone distinct of all that company,
you went on, you went on,
into the darkness;
and I sit here at my table,
holding back my tears,
with my jaw set and my teeth clenched,
knowing I shall not be
even so near you as I saw you
in my dream.

F. S. Flint

ABOVE: *The Worcester regiment, 11 November 1916*

RIGHT: *Fricourt, 18 October 1917*

MY BROTHER

Translated from the Arabic by Sharif S. Elmusa and Gregory Orfalea

Brother, if on the heels of war Western man celebrates his deeds,
Consecrates the memory of the fallen and builds monuments for heroes,
Do not yourself sing for the victors nor rejoice over those trampled by
    victorious wheels;
Rather kneel as I do, wounded, for the end of our dead.

Brother, if after the war a soldier comes home
And throws his tired body into the arms of friends,
Do not hope on your return for friends.
Hunger struck down all to whom we might whisper our pain.

Brother, if the farmer returns to till his land,
And after long exile rebuilds a shack which cannon had wrecked,
Our waterwheels have dried up
And the foes have left no seedling except the scattered corpses.

Brother, misery nestled everywhere – through our will.
Do not lament. Others do not hear our woe.
Instead follow me with a pick and spade that we may dig a trench in which
    to hide our dead.

Dear brother, who are we without a neighbour, kin or country?
We sleep and we wake clad in shame.

The world breathes our stench, as it did that of the dead.
Bring the spade and follow me – dig another trench for those still alive.

Mikhail Naimy

ABOVE: *Chinese workers drafted in to make munitions for the French*

RIGHT: *Migrant workers employed in the French construction industry*

MANY SISTERS TO MANY BROTHERS

When we fought campaigns (in the long Christmas rains)

With soldiers spread in troops on the floor,

I shot as straight as you, my losses were as few,

My victories as many, or more.

And when in naval battle, amid cannon's rattle,

Fleet met fleet in the bath,

My cruisers were as trim, my battleships as grim,

My submarines cut as swift a path.

Or, when it rained too long, and the strength of the strong

Surged up and broke a way with blows,

I was as fit and keen, my fists hit as clean,

Your black eye matched my bleeding nose.

Was there a scrap or ploy in which you, the boy,

Could better me? You could not climb higher,

Ride straighter, run as quick (and to smoke made you sick)

…But I sit here and you're under fire.

Oh, it's you that have the luck, out there in blood and muck:

You were born beneath a kindly star;

All we dreamt, I and you, you can really go and do,

And I can't, the way things are.

In a trench you are sitting, while I am knitting

A hopeless sock that never gets done.

Well, here's luck, my dear; – and you've got it, no fear;

But for me … a war is poor fun.

Rose Macaulay

ABOVE: *Red Cross workers assist the wounded on no man's land*

LEFT: *September 1918: US troops arrive in France*

55

ULTIMA RATIO REGUM

The guns spell money's ultimate reason
In letters of lead on the Spring hillside.
But the boy lying dead under the olive trees
Was too young and too silly
To have been notable to their important eye.
He was a better target for a kiss.

When he lived, tall factory hooters never summoned him
Nor did restaurant plate-glass doors revolve to wave him in.
His name never appeared in the papers.
The world maintained its traditional wall
Round the dead with their gold sunk deep as a well,
Whilst his life, intangible as a Stock Exchange rumour,
    drifted outside.

O too lightly he threw down his cap
One day when the breeze threw petals from the trees.
The unflowering wall sprouted with guns,
Machine-gun anger quickly scythed the grasses;
Flags and leaves fell from hands and branches;
The tweed cap rotted in the nettles.

Consider his life which was valueless
In terms of employment, hotel ledgers, new files.
Consider. One bullet in ten thousand kills a man.
Ask. Was so much expenditure justified
On the death of one so young, and so silly
Lying under the olive trees, O world, O death?

Stephen Spender

ABOVE: *German soldiers left behind after a battle, 12 October 1917*

LEFT: *Trees damaged by shells are used for roads, bridges and dug-outs*

IN THE AMBULANCE

Two rows of cabbages,
Two of curly-greens,
Two rows of early peas,
Two of kidney-beans.

That's what he keeps muttering,
Making such a song,
Keeping other chaps awake
The whole night long.

Both his legs are shot away,
And his head is light,
So he keeps on muttering
All the blessed night:

Two rows of cabbages,
Two of curly-greens,
Two rows of early peas,
Two of kidney-beans.

Wilfrid Gibson

RIGHT: *Injured soldiers wheeled to makeshift hospitals*

BELOW: *A column from the East Yorkshire Regiment march into battle*

A THRUSH IN THE TRENCHES

(from The Soldier)

Suddenly he sang across the trenches,
vivid in the fleeting hush
as a star-shell through the smashed black branches,
a more than English thrush.

Suddenly he sang, and those who listened
nor moved nor wondered, but
heard, all bewitched, the sweet unhastened
crystal Magnificat.

One crouched, a muddied rifle clasping,
and one a filled grenade,
but little cared they, while he went lisping
the one clear tune he had.

Paused horror, hate and Hell a moment,
(you could almost hear the sigh)
and still he sang to them, and so went
(suddenly) singing by.

Humbert Wolfe

FAR LEFT: *15 December 1916: the Battle of Verdun has finally ended*

LEFT: *Preparing bayonets for attack*

THE SOLDIER

If I should die, think only this of me:
That there's some corner of a foreign field
That is for ever England. There shall be
In that rich earth a richer dust concealed;
A dust whom England bore, shaped, made aware,
Gave, once, her flowers to love, her ways to roam,
A body of England's, breathing English air,
Washed by the rivers, blest by suns of home.

And think, this heart, all evil shed away,
A pulse in the eternal mind, no less
Gives somewhere back the thoughts by England given;
Her sights and sounds; dreams happy as her day;
And laughter, learnt of friends; and gentleness,
In hearts at peace, under an English heaven.

ABOVE: *Sixty-pound field guns in action at Arras*

Rupert Brooke

THE MOTHER

If you should die, think only this of me
In that still quietness where is space for thought,
Where parting, loss and bloodshed shall not be,
And men may rest themselves and dream of nought:
That in some place a mystic mile away
One whom you loved has drained the bitter cup
Till there is nought to drink; has faced the day
Once more, and now, has raised the standard up.

And think, my son, with eyes grown clear and dry
She lives as though for ever in your sight,
Loving the things *you* loved, with heart aglow
For country, honour, truth, traditions high,
– Proud that you paid their price. (And if some night
Her heart should break – well, lad, you will not know.)

May Herschel-Clark

ABOVE: *Birmingham 1918: a woman takes control of the railway signals*

BELOW: *Nurses tend a wounded soldier on the western front*

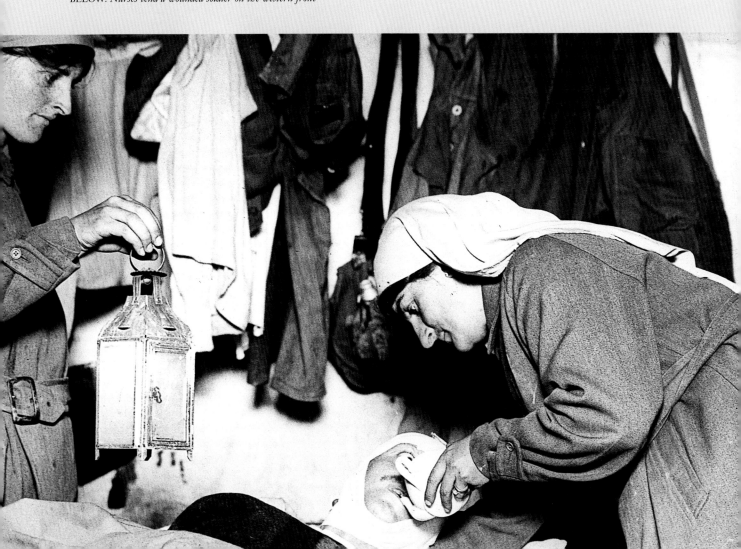

A WAR FILM

I saw,
With a catch of the breath and the heart's uplifting,
Sorrow and pride,
The 'week's great draw' –
The Mons Retreat;
The 'Old Contemptibles' who fought, and died,
The horror and the anguish and the glory.

As in a dream,
Still hearing machine-guns rattle and shells scream,
I came out into the street.

When day was done,
My little son
Wondered at bath-time why I kissed him so,
Naked upon my knee.
How could he know
The sudden terror that assaulted me? ...
The body I had borne
Nine moons beneath my heart,
A part of me ...
If, someday,
It should be taken away
To War. Tortured. Torn.
Slain.

Rotting in No Man's Land, out in the rain –
My little son ...
Yet all those men had mothers, every one.

How should he know
Why I kissed and kissed and kissed him, crooning his
     name?
He thought that I was daft.
He thought it was a game,
And laughed, and laughed.

Theresa Hooley

ABOVE: *Howitzer guns, 1916*

BELOW: *6 July 1916: the first day of the Battle of the Somme*

THOSE WHO WAIT

Who knows the thots of mothers who wait,
Whether in grandeur, or lowly state;
Who knows the sacrifice of those who give,
Their all, their sons, that we might live?

The days are long as I sit here and knit,
Fashioning these socks for him ... bit by bit;
My thots are ever one constant prayer,
For my boy, my all, who is 'Over There.'

The long endless nights bring no rest,
My baby again nestles close to my breast;
Sense of his touch brings sweet poignant joy,
'May God watch o'er him, my own ... my boy.'

Was only a lad, but then he would go,
I'm heartsick dear Lord, proud of him tho,
Our country needed, he heard the call,
Light's gone from life, for he is my all.

Watching the mail box here by the gate,
For I know not what, I wait and wait ...
Body's a-sweat with fevered chill,
When postman stops, my heart stands still.

'Our boys gained, advanced to Meuse,
Will advance beyond,' so reads the news;
And in glowing terms they praise our men,
But I'm gripped in throes of that fear again.

Wait 'till the last before I look at the list,
The words go blur as my eyes grow mist,
I'm stifled and choked with that nameless
    dread,
Of seeing *his* name among the dead.

Who knows the thots of mothers who wait,
Whether in grandeur, or lowly state;
Who knows the sacrifice of those who give,
Their all, their sons, that we might live?

from *Rhymes of a*
Lost Battalion Doughboy

ABOVE: *Families reunited*

RIGHT: *Outside the War Office on the eve of the war*

MOTHERS

In the still of night
Have we wept.
And our hearts, shattered and aching
Have prayed.
In the cold, cold moonlight
Have we sobbed
And dreamed of what might have been.
And our hearts have bled from stabs
Given unheeding.
We are the women who have suffered alone –
Alone and in silence.

ABOVE: *A garden party in aid of blind soldiers*

Kay Boyle

GRASS

ABOVE: *The dead left in the trenches*

BELOW: *The battle of Vimy Ridge, April 1917*

Pile the bodies high at Austerlitz and Waterloo.
Shovel them under and let me work –
I am the grass; I cover all.

And pile them high at Gettysburg
And pile them high at Ypres and Verdun.
Shovel them under and let me work.
Two years, ten years, and passengers ask the conductor:
What place is this?
Where are we now?

I am the grass.
Let me work.

Carl Sandburg

THE SILENT ONE

Who died on the wires, and hung there, one of two –
Who for his hours of life has chattered through
Infinite lovely chatter of Bucks accent;
Yet faced unbroken wires; stepped over, and went,
A noble fool, faithful to his stripes – and ended.
But I weak, hungry, and willing only for the chance
Of line – to fight in the line, lay down under unbroken
Wires, and saw the flashes, and kept unshaken.
Till the politest voice – a finicking accent, said:
'Do you think you might crawl through, there; there's a hole'
Darkness, shot at; I smiled, as politely replied –
'I'm afraid not, Sir.' There was no hole, no way to be seen.
Nothing but chance of death, after tearing of clothes.
Kept flat, and watched the darkness, hearing bullets whizzing –
And thought of music – and swore deep heart's deep oaths
(Polite to God –) and retreated and came on again.
Again retreated – and a second time faced the screen.

Ivor Gurney

TOP: *German Red Cross members collect casualties*

ABOVE: *Western front, 27 December 1916*

THE KITCHENER CHAP

He wore twin stripes of gold upon
An empty tunic sleeve;
His eyes were blue, his face so young
One hardly could believe
That he had seen the death and hate
That make the whole word grieve.

His hair was fair, his eyes were blue,
I thought that I could see
(Just when his sunny smile came through)
The lad he used to be:
Dear happy little mother's lad
Of only two or three.

But when across his eyes there came
A sudden look of pain –
His mouth set very hard and straight,
He was a man again.
He gave his shattered dreams of youth
That England might remain.

I felt hot tears rise to my eyes
When I looked at the lad;
Brave, gallant, shattered, smiling youth –
He gave us all he had;
For youth so fair, so sorely hurt
All England's heart is sad.

He passed me on a crowded street,
We did not meet again;
He showed me in a sudden flash
Our England's pride and pain.
And when all is long forgot
His memory shall remain.

Horace Bray

LEFT & ABOVE: *Lord Kitchener, Secretary of State for War*

STRANGE MEETING

It seemed that out of the battle I escaped
Down some profound dull tunnel, long since scooped
Through granites which Titanic wars had groined.
Yet also there encumbered sleepers groaned,
Too fast in thought or death to be bestirred.
Then, as I probed them, one sprang up, and stared
With piteous recognition in fixed eyes,
Lifting distressful hands as if to bless.
And by his smile, I knew that sullen hall,
By his dead smile I knew we stood in Hell.
With a thousand pains that vision's face was grained;
Yet no blood reached there from the upper ground,
And no guns thumped, or down the flues made
   moan.
'Strange, friend,' I said, 'here is no cause to mourn.'
'None,' said that other, 'save the undone years,
The hopelessness. Whatever hope is yours,
Was my life also; I went hunting wild
After the wildest beauty in the world,
Which lies not calm in eyes, or braided hair,
But mocks the steady running of the hour,
And if it grieves, grieves richlier than here.
For of my glee might many men have laughed,
And of my weeping something has been left,
Which must die now. I mean the truth untold,
The pity of war, the pity war distilled.

Now men will go content with what we spoiled,
Or, discontent, boil bloody, and be spilled.
They will be swift with swiftness of the tigress,
None will break ranks, though nations trek from
   progress.
Courage was mine, and I had mystery,
Wisdom was mine, and I had mastery:
To miss the march of this retreating world
Into vain citadels that are not walled.
Then, when much blood had clogged their chariot-
   wheels
I would go up and wash them from sweet wells,
Even with truths that lie too deep for taint.
I would have poured my spirit without stint
But not through wounds; not on the cess of war.
Foreheads of men have bled where no wounds were.
I am the enemy you killed, my friend.
I knew you in this dark; for so you frowned
Yesterday through me as you jabbed and killed.
I parried; but my hands were loath and cold.
Let us sleep now....'

Wilfred Owen

ABOVE: *19 July 1916*

RIGHT: *A helping hand for a wounded soldier*

'I TRACKED A DEAD MAN DOWN A TRENCH'

I tracked a dead man down a trench,
I knew not he was dead.
They told me he had gone that way,
And there his foot-marks led.

The trench was long and close and curved,
It seemed without an end;
And as I threaded each new bay
I thought to see my friend.

I went there stooping to the ground.
For, should I raise my head,
Death watched to spring; and how should then
A dead man find the dead?

At last I saw his back. He crouched
As still as still could be,
And when I called his name aloud
He did not answer me.

The floor-way of the trench was wet
Where he was crouching dead:
The water of the pool was brown,
And round him it was red.

I stole up softly where he stayed
With head hung down all slack,
And on his shoulders laid my hands
And drew him gently back.

And then, as I had guessed, I saw
His head, and how the crown –
I saw then why he crouched so still
And why his head hung down.

W. S. S. Lyon

RIGHT: *Canadians go over the top*

BELOW: *A British soldier sits in quiet contemplation, autumn 1917*

A STORY OF TODAY

An open drawer, a woman lowly kneeling,
Some little crimson shoes, a lock of hair,
Some childish toys, an engine and a trumpet,
A headless horse, a battered Teddy bear.
Some school-boy books, all inky, torn and thumb-marked,
A treasured bat, his favourite cricket ball,
The things he loved, the letters that he wrote her –
And now she places on the top of all
A soldier's sword, his photograph, in khaki –
The boyish eyes smile back into her eyes,
While in her hand she holds a V.C. tightly,
And in her heart a grave in Flanders lies.

Constance Powell

ABOVE: *A lone soldier crosses a makeshift bridge*

THE CHERRY TREES

The cherry trees bend over and are shedding,
On the old road where all that passed are dead,
Their petals, strewing the grass as for a wedding
This early May morn when there is none to wed.

Edward Thomas

ABOVE: *Delville Woods, often referred to as 'Devil's Wood' by British soldiers*

LEFT: *14 October 1917*

THE HERO

'Jack fell as he'd have wished,' the Mother said,
And folded up the letter that she'd read.
'The Colonel writes so nicely.' Something broke
In the tired voice that quavered to a choke.
She half looked up. 'We mothers are so proud
Of our dead soldiers.' Then her face was bowed.

Quietly the Brother Officer went out.
He'd told the poor old dear some gallant lies
That she would nourish all her days, no doubt.
For while he coughed and mumbled, her weak eyes
Had shone with gentle triumph, brimmed with joy,
Because he'd been so brave, her glorious boy.

He thought how 'Jack', cold-footed, useless swine,
Had panicked down the trench that night the mine
Went up at Wicked Corner; how he'd tried
To get sent home, and how, at last, he died,
Blown to small bits. And no one seemed to care
Except that lonely woman with white hair.

Siegfried Sassoon

RIGHT: *A Red Cross flag flies above the advanced dressing station*

BELOW: *Nurses lay tributes at the foot of a soldier's grave*

THE DESERTER

'I'm sorry I done it, Major.'
We bandaged the livid face;
And led him, ere the wan sun rose,
To die his death of disgrace.

The bolt-heads locked to the cartridge;
The rifles steadied to rest,
As cold stock nestled at colder cheek
And foresight lined on the breast.

'*Fire!*' called the Sergeant-Major.
The muzzles flamed as he spoke:
And the shameless soul of a nameless man
Went up in the cordite-smoke.

Gilbert Frankau

ABOVE: *Infantrymen on the eve of the Somme offensive*

BELOW: *Western Front, December 1916*

BULLY BEEF

ABOVE: *29 November 1917*

BELOW: *A girl sells oranges to passing troops in Flanders*

Have you ever had your stomach,
In a mass of whirlin' pain,
While 'doing your bit' Over There,
In the drippin' ice-cold rain.

With the mud up to your knee-caps,
And your shoes a-slushin' 'round,
On your way up to the front again,
Tired as a wind-broke hound.

Had your Serg' come runnin' yelling,
'Here comes the ration truck,'
You grabbed a can of Bully Beef,
Then sat right down in the muck.

Madly tore the tough old lid off,
With your bayonet's rusty blade,
Gulped it down in great big chunks,
And cared not how it's made.

It ironed out all the wrinkles,
And for the likes of you and me,
'Twas *Bully Beef* who licked the Kaiser,
And he earned a D.S.C.

from *Rhymes of
a Lost Battalion Doughboy*

RETURNING, WE HEAR THE LARKS

Sombre the night is.
And though we have our lives, we know
What sinister threat lurks there.

Dragging these anguished limbs, we only know
This poison-blasted track opens on our camp –
On a little safe sleep.

But hark! joy – joy – strange joy.
Lo! heights of night ringing with unseen larks.
Music showering on our upturned list'ning faces.

Death could drop from the dark
As easily as song –
But song only dropped,
Like a blind man's dreams on the sand
By dangerous tides,
Like a girl's dark hair for she dreams no ruin lies there,
Or her kisses where a serpent hides.

Isaac Rosenberg

ABOVE: *A newly constructed bridge*

BELOW: *British troops at Verneuil, 29 May 1918*

LIGHTS OUT

I have come to the borders of sleep,
The unfathomable deep
Forest where all must lose
Their way, however straight,
Or winding, soon or late;
They cannot choose.

Many a road and track
That, since the dawn's first crack,
Up to the forest brink,
Deceived the travellers,
Suddenly now blurs,
And in they sink.

Here love ends,
Despair, ambition ends,
All pleasure and all trouble,
Although most sweet or bitter,
Here ends in sleep that is sweeter
Than tasks most noble.

There is not any book
Or face of dearest look
That I would not turn from now
To go into the unknown
I must enter and leave alone
I know not how.

The tall forest towers;
Its cloudy foliage lowers
Ahead, shelf above shelf;
Its silence I hear and obey
That I may lose my way
And myself.

Edward Thomas

RIGHT: *Much-needed sleep for the Royal Warwickshire Regiment*

BELOW: *The remains of battlefields on the western front*

A SHROPSHIRE LAD: XI

On your midnight pallet lying,
Listen, and undo the door:
Lads that waste the light in sighing
In the dark should sigh no more;
Night should ease a lover's sorrow;
Therefore, since I go to-morrow,
Pity me before.

In the land to which I travel,
The far dwelling, let me say —
Once, if here the couch is gravel,
In a kinder bed I lay,
And the breast the darnel smothers
Rested once upon another's
When it was not clay.

TOP: *An ammunition column at the Battle of Cambrai
24 November 1917*

ABOVE: *British cavalry, 21 November 1917*

A. E. Housman

LIGHT AFTER DARKNESS

Once more the Night, like some great dark drop-scene
Eclipsing horrors for a brief *entr'acte*,
Descends, lead-weighty. Now the space between,
Fringed with the eager eyes of men, is racked
By spark-tailed lights, curvetting far and high,
Swift smoke-flecked coursers, raking the black sky.

And as each sinks in ashes grey, one more
Rises to fall, and so through all the hours
They strive like petty empires by the score,
Each confident of its success and powers,
And, hovering at its zenith, each will show
Pale, rigid faces, lying dead, below.

There shall they lie, tainting the innocent air,
Until the dawn, deep veiled in mournful grey,
Sadly and quietly shall lay them bare,
The broken heralds of a doleful day.

E. Wyndham Tennant

ABOVE: *Canadian stretcher party, November 1917*

BELOW: *A German victim from the 242nd Regiment*

'BOMBED LAST NIGHT'

ABOVE: *A trench dressing station*

BELOW: *The aftermath of Flanders*

Bombed last night, and bombed the night before.
Going to get bombed tonight if we never get bombed
    any more.
When we're bombed, we're scared as we can be.
Can't stop the bombing from old Higher Germany.

They're warning us, they're warning us.
One shell hole for just the four of us.
Thank your lucky stars there are no more of us.
So one of us can fill it all alone.

Gassed last night, and gassed the night before.
Going to get gassed tonight if we never get gassed
    any more.
When we're gassed, we're sick as we can be.
For phosgene and mustard gas is much too much
    for me.

They're killing us, they're killing us.
One respirator for the four of us.
Thank your lucky stars that we can all run fast.
So one of us can take it all alone.

Soldiers' song

CLEARING-STATION

Translated from the German by Patrick Bridgwater

Straw rustling everywhere.
The candle-stumps stand there staring solemnly.
Across the nocturnal vault of the church
Moans go drifting and choking words.

There's a stench of blood, pus, shit and sweat.
Bandages ooze away underneath torn uniforms.
Clammy trembling hands and wasted faces.
Bodies stay propped up as their dying heads slump
    down.

In the distance the battle thunders grimly on,
Day and night, groaning and grumbling non-stop,
And to the dying men patiently waiting for their graves
It sounds for all the world like the words of God.

Wilhelm Klemm

ABOVE: *Stretcher bearers in Flanders*

BELOW: *A comrade lifts a wounded soldier to safety*

FIELD AMBULANCE IN RETREAT

VIA DOLOROSA, VIA SACRA

I

A straight flagged road, laid on the rough earth,
A causeway of stone from beautiful city to city,
Between the tall trees, the slender, delicate trees,
Through the flat green land, by plots of flowers, by
    black canals thick with heat.

II

The road-makers made it well
Of fine stone, strong for the feet of the oxen and the
    great Flemish horses,
And for the high wagons piled with corn from the
    harvest.
And the labourers are few;
They and their quiet oxen stand aside and wait
By the long road loud with the passing of guns, the
    rush of armoured cars, and the tramp of an army on
    the march forward to battle;
And, where the piled corn-wagons went, our dripping
    Ambulance carries home
Its red and white harvest from the fields.

III

The straight flagged road breaks into dust, into a thin
    white cloud,
About the feet of a regiment driven back league by
    league,
Rifles at trail, and standards wrapped in black funeral
    cloths. Unhasting, proud in retreat,
They smile as the Red Cross Ambulance rushes by.
(You know nothing of beauty and desolation who have
    not seen
That smile of an army in retreat.)
They go: and our shining, beckoning danger goes with
    them,

And our joy in the harvests that we gathered in at
    nightfall in the fields;
And like an unloved hand laid on a beating heart
Our safety wears us down.
Safety hard and strange; stranger and yet more hard,
As, league after dying league, the beautiful, desolate
    Land
Falls back from the intolerable speed of an Ambulance
    in retreat
On the sacred, dolorous Way.

May Sinclair

RIGHT: *The remains of Delville Wood after a six-day battle*

CHAMPS D'HONNEUR

Soldiers never do die well;
Crosses mark the places,
Wooden crosses where they fell;
Stuck above their faces.
Soldiers pitch and cough and twitch;
All the world roars red and black,
Soldiers smother in a ditch;
Choking through the whole attack.

Ernest Hemingway

RIGHT: *Tending Canadian graves*

'I WANT TO GO HOME'

I want to go home, I want to go home.
I don't want to go in the trenches no more,
Where whizzbangs and shrapnel they whistle and roar.
Take me over the sea, where the Alleyman can't get at me.
Oh my, I don't want to die, I want to go home.

I want to go home, I want to go home.
I don't want to visit la Belle France no more,
For oh the Jack Johnsons they make such a roar.
Take me over the sea, where the snipers they can't get at me.
Oh my, I don't want to die, I want to go home.

Soldiers' song

ABOVE LEFT: *Troops collected after fighting at Arras*

LEFT: *Spring 1918*

IN A SOLDIERS' HOSPITAL I: PLUCK

Crippled for life at seventeen,
His great eyes seem to question why:
With both legs smashed it might have been
Better in that grim trench to die
Than drag maimed years out helplessly.

A child – so wasted and so white,
He told a lie to get his way,
To march, a man with men, and fight
While other boys are still at play.
A gallant lie your heart will say.

So broke with pain, he shrinks in dread
To see the 'dresser' drawing near;
And winds the clothes about his head
That none may see his heart-sick fear.
His shaking, strangled sobs you hear.

But when the dreaded moment's there
He'll face us all, a soldier yet,
Watch his bared wounds with unmoved air,
(Though tell-tale lashes still are wet)
And smoke his woodbine cigarette.

Eva Dobell

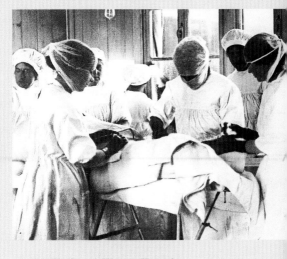

ABOVE: *The Scottish Women's Hospital*

BELOW: *A Voluntary Aid Detachment nurse tends a wounded soldier*

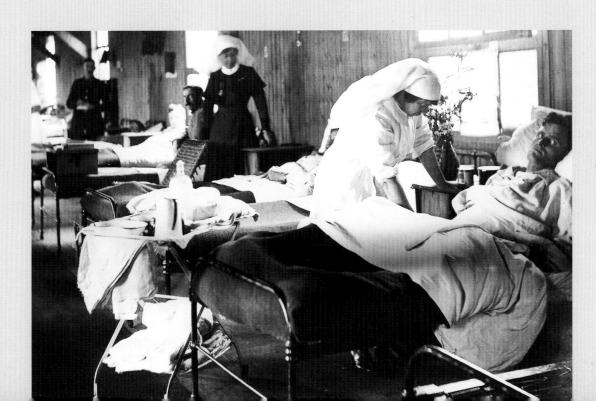

THE VETERAN

We came upon him sitting in the sun,
Blinded by war, and left. And past the fence
There came young soldiers from the *Hand and Flower*,
Asking advice of his experience.

And he said this, and that, and told them tales,
And all the nightmares of each empty head
Blew into air; then, hearing us beside,
'Poor chaps, how'd they know what it's like?' he said.

We stood there, and watched him as he sat,
Turning his sockets where they went away,
Until it came to one of us to ask
'And you're – how old?'
'Nineteen, the third of May.'

Margaret Postgate Cole

ABOVE: *Soldiers enter Lille, October 1918*

BELOW: *On guard in a forward trench*

TO THE WARMONGERS

I'm back again from hell
With loathsome thoughts to sell;
Secrets of death to tell;
And horrors from the abyss.
Young faces bleared with blood,
Sucked down into the mud,
You shall hear things like this,
Till the tormented slain
Crawl round and once again,
With limbs that twist awry
Moan out their brutish pain,
As the fighters pass them by.
For you our battles shine
With triumph half-divine;
And the glory of the dead
Kindles in each proud eye.
But a curse is on my head,
That shall not be unsaid,
And the wounds in my heart are red,
For I have watched them die.

Siegfried Sassoon

ABOVE: *9 April 1918*

THE FALLING LEAVES

November 1915

Today, as I rode by,
I saw the brown leaves dropping from their tree
In a still afternoon,
When no wind whirled them whistling to the sky,
But thickly, silently,
They fell, like snowflakes wiping out the noon;
And wandered slowly thence
For thinking of a gallant multitude
Which now all withering lay,
Slain by no wind of age or pestilence,
But in their beauty strewed
Like snowflakes falling on the Flemish clay.

Margaret Postgate Cole

RIGHT: *The Somme, 1916*

ANTHEM FOR DOOMED YOUTH

What passing-bells for these who die as cattle?
Only the monstrous anger of the guns.
Only the stuttering rifles' rapid rattle
Can patter out their hasty orisons.
No mockeries now for them; no prayers nor bells,
Nor any voice of mourning save the choirs, –
The shrill, demented choirs of wailing shells;
And bugles calling for them from sad shires.

What candles may be held to speed them all?
Not in the hands of boys, but in their eyes
Shall shine the holy glimmers of goodbyes.
The pallor of girls' brows shall be their pall;
Their flowers the tenderness of patient minds,
And each slow dusk a drawing-down of blinds.

Wilfred Owen

ABOVE: *The Welsh Guard at Guillemont*

BELOW: *Wounded are taken to a farmhouse hospital station*

THE MEDAL

'Tis not the bit of bronze and metal,
That tells the time-worn tale,
Of some act of heroism
Where bullets whine and wail.

Nor are the colored ribbons,
Pinned on some strutting chest,
Always truthful indicators,
Of the men who fought the best.

Nor do gold stripes upon the arm
Always tell the story,
Of men who have seen action
Or fought their way to glory.

These are outward indications
Made by the hand of man,
Way they're sometimes passed about,
Is hard to understand.

They will tarnish with the weather,
In the plush or on the shelf,
For the real and lasting medal,
Is the soul within yourself.

Did you do your best when called on,
In the air or torn shell-hole,
You've got some real satisfaction,
Buried deep within your soul.

No bit of bronze or ribbon bright,
Or words of praise high spoken,
Can change the thots that lie within,
They are the genuine tokens.

Telling the tale as long as you live,
And the truth of how you fought,
If you played the game with all you had,
You've the medal that can't be bought.

from *Rhymes of a
Lost Battalion Doughboy*

ABOVE: *Reinforcements move up towards Flers*

RIGHT: *An Australian Imperial Guard keeps watch*

DISABLED

He sat in a wheeled chair, waiting for dark,
And shivered in his ghastly suit of grey,
Legless, sewn short at elbow. Through the park
Voices of boys rang saddening like a hymn,
Voices of play and pleasure after day,
Till gathering sleep had mothered them from him.

About this time Town used to swing so gay
When glow-lamps budded in the light blue trees
And girls glanced lovelier as the air grew dim, –
In the old times, before he threw away his knees.
Now he will never feel again how slim
Girls' waists are, nor how warm their subtle hands,
All of them touch him like some queer disease.

There was an artist silly for his face,
For it was younger than his youth, last year.
Now, he is old; his back will never brace;
He's lost his colour very far from here,
Poured it down shell-holes till the veins ran dry,
And half his lifetime lapsed in the hot race,
And leap of purple spurted from his thigh.

One time he liked a bloodsmear down his leg,
After the matches, carried shoulder-high.
It was after football, when he'd drunk a peg,
He thought he'd better join. – He wonders why …
Someone had said he'd look a god in kilts.

That's why; and maybe, too, to please his Meg,
Aye, that was it, to please the giddy jilts
He asked to join. He didn't have to beg;
Smiling they wrote his lie; aged nineteen years.
Germans he scarcely thought of; all their guilt,
And Austria's, did not move him. And no fears
Of Fear came yet. He thought of jewelled hilts
For daggers in plaid socks; of smart salutes;
And care of arms; and leave; and pay arrears;
Esprit de corps; and hints for young recruits.
And soon, he was drafted out with drums and cheers.

Some cheered him home, but not as crowds cheer Goal.
Only a solemn man who brought him fruits
Thanked him; and then inquired about his soul.

Now, he will spend a few sick years in Institutes,
And do what things the rules consider wise,
And take whatever pity they may dole.
To-night he noticed how the women's eyes
Passed from him to the strong men that were whole.
How cold and late it is! Why don't they come
And put him into bed? Why don't they come?

Wilfred Owen

BELOW: *The British attack Arras, 9 April 1917*

From HUGH SELWYN MAUBERLEY

(Life and contacts)

These fought in any case,
and some believing,
pro domo, in any case …

Some quick to arm,
some for adventure,
some from fear of weakness,
some from fear of censure,
some for love of slaughter, in imagination,
learning later ….
some in fear, learning love of slaughter;
Died some, pro patria,
non 'dulce' non 'et decor' …
walked eye-deep in hell
believing in old men's lies, then unbelieving
came home, home to a lie,
home to many deceits,
home to old lies and new infamy;
usury age-old and age-thick
and liars in public places.

Daring as never before, wastage as never before.
Young blood and high blood,
fair cheeks, and fine bodies;
fortitude as never before

frankness as never before,
disillusions as never told in the old days,
hysterias, trench confessions,
laughter out of dead bellies.

There died a myriad,
And of the best, among them,
For an old bitch gone in the teeth,
For a botched civilization,

Charm, smiling at the good mouth,
Quick eyes gone under earth's lid,

For two gross broken statues,
For a few thousand battered books.

Ezra Pound

ABOVE: *The remains of Peronne Cathedral*

RIGHT: *Statues rescued from Arras Cathedral*

NOT TO KEEP

They sent him back to her. The letter came
Saying … And she could have him. And before
She could be sure there was no hidden ill
Under the formal writing, he was in her sight,
Living. They gave him back to her alive –
How else? They are not known to send the dead
–
And not disfigured visibly. His face?
His hands? She had to look, to ask,
'What is it, dear?' And she had given all
And still she had all – *they* had – they the lucky!
Wasn't she glad now? Everything seemed won,
And all the rest for them permissible ease.
She had to ask, 'What was it, dear?'
'Enough,

Yet not enough. A bullet through and through,
High in the breast. Nothing but what good care
And medicine and rest, and you a week,
Can cure me of to go again.' The same
Grim giving to do over for them both.
She dared no more than ask him with her eyes
How was it with him for a second trial.
And with his eyes he asked her not to ask.
They had given him back to her, but not to keep.

Robert Frost

RIGHT: *Shells explode near a British soldier*

BELOW: *Wounded soldiers arrive at Ostend, autumn 1914*

LAMPLIGHT

We planned to shake the world together, you and I
Being young, and very wise;
Now in the light of the green shaded lamp
Almost I see your eyes
Light with the old gay laughter; you and I
Dreamed greatly of an Empire in those days,
Setting our feet upon laborious ways,
And all you asked of fame
Was crossed swords in the Army List,
My Dear, against your name.

We planned a great Empire together, you and I,
Bound only by the sea;
Now in the quiet of a chill Winter's night
Your voice comes hushed to me
Full of forgotten memories: you and I
Dreamed great dreams of our future in those days,
Setting our feet on undiscovered ways,
And all I asked of fame
A scarlet cross on my breast, my Dear,
For the swords by your name.

We shall never shake the world together, you and I,
For you gave your life away;
And I think my heart was broken by the war,
Since on a summer day
You took the road we never spoke of: you and I
Dreamed greatly of an Empire in those days;
You set your feet upon the Western ways
And have no need of fame –
There's a scarlet cross on my breast, my Dear,
And a torn cross with your name.

May Wedderburn Cannan

ABOVE: *A brigadier-general waits on his troops, 29 December 1917*

RIGHT: *Women in the Royal Naval Service were nicknamed 'Jenny Wrens'.*

ON ACTIVE SERVICE

American Expeditionary Force (R.S., August 12th, 1918)

He is dead that was alive.
How shall friendship understand?
Lavish heart and tireless hand
Bidden not to give or strive,
Eager brain and questing eye
Like a broken lens laid by.

He, with so much left to do,
Such a gallant race to run,
What concern had he with you,
Silent Keeper of things done?

Tell us not that, wise and young,
Elsewhere he lives out his plan.
Our speech was sweetest to his tongue,
And his great gift was to be man.

Long and long shall we remember,
In our breasts his grave be made.
It shall never be December
Where so warm a heart is laid,
But in our saddest selves a sweet voice sing,
Recalling him, and Spring.

Edith Wharton

ABOVE: *The fallen after the Battle of Marne, September 1914*

RIGHT: *Peronne Square after the German withdrawal*

MENTAL CASES

Who are these? Why sit they here in twilight?
Wherefore rock they, purgatorial shadows,
Drooping tongues from jaws that slob their relish,
Baring teeth that leer like skulls' teeth wicked?
Stroke on stroke of pain, – but what slow panic,
Gouged these chasms round their fretted sockets?
Ever from their hair and through their hands' palms
Misery swelters. Surely we have perished
Sleeping, and walk hell; but who these hellish?

– These are men whose minds the Dead have
    ravished.
Memory fingers in their hair of murders,
Multitudinous murders they once witnessed.
Wading sloughs of flesh these helpless wander,
Treading blood from lungs that had loved laughter.
Always they must see these things and hear them,
Batter of guns and shatter of flying muscles,
Carnage incomparable and human squander
Rucked too thick for these men's extrication.

Therefore still their eyeballs shrink tormented
Back into their brains, because on their sense
Sunlight seems a bloodsmear; night comes blood-
    black;
Dawn breaks open like a wound that bleeds afresh.
– Thus their heads wear this hilarious, hideous,
Awful falseness of set-smiling corpses.
– Thus their hands are plucking at each other;
Picking at the rope-knouts of their scourging;
Snatching after us who smote them, brother,
Pawing us who dealt them war and madness.

Wilfred Owen

RIGHT: *Shellburst near an advanced dressing station*

BELOW: *Advanced dressing station on the western front*

IN A SOLDIERS' HOSPITAL II: GRAMOPHONE TUNES

Through the long ward the gramophone
Grinds out its nasal melodies:
'Where did you get that girl?' it shrills.
The patients listen at their ease,
Through clouds of strong tobacco-smoke:
The gramophone can always please.

The Welsh boy has it by his bed,
(He's lame – one leg was blown away.)
He'll lie propped up with pillows there,
And wind the handle half the day.
His neighbour, with the shattered arm,
Picks out the records he must play.

Jock with his crutches beats the time;
The gunner, with his head close-bound,
Listens with puzzled, patient smile:
(Shell-shock – he cannot hear a sound.)
The others join in from their beds,
And send the chorus rolling round.

Somehow for me these common tunes
Can never sound the same again:
They've magic now to thrill my heart
And bring before me, clear and plain,
Man that is master of his flesh,
And has the laugh of death and pain.

Eva Dobell

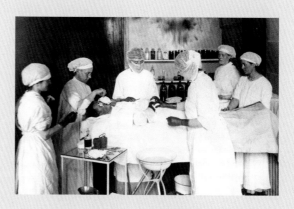

ABOVE: *An emergency theatre set up behind the front line*

BELOW: *Wounded soldiers safely back in English hospitals to recover*

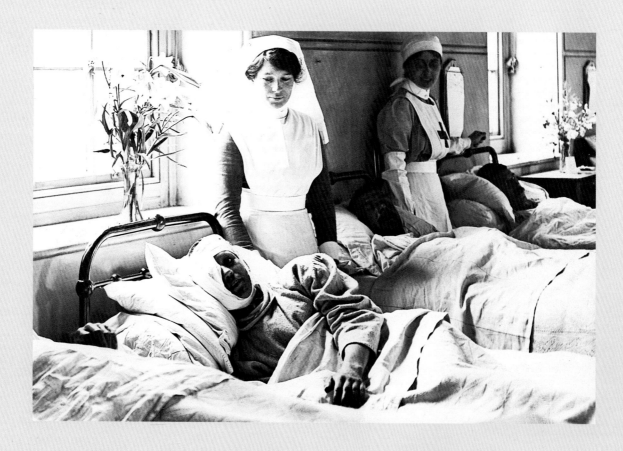

A MEMORY

There was no sound at all, no crying in the village,
Nothing you would count as sound, that is, after the
    shells;
Only behind a wall the slow sobbing of women,
The creaking of a door, a lost dog – nothing else.

Silence which might be felt, no pity in the silence,
Horrible, soft like blood, down all the blood-stained
    ways;
In the middle of the street two corpses lie unburied,
And a bayoneted woman stares in the market-place.

Humble and ruined folk – for these no pride of
    conquest,
Their only prayer: 'O! Lord, give us our daily
    bread!'
Not by the battle fires, the shrapnel are we haunted;
Who shall deliver us from the memory of these
    dead?

Margaret Sackville

TOP: *French villagers rescued from German occupation welcome the British troops*

ABOVE: *French towns were gradually liberated*

MAY, 1915

Let us remember Spring will come again
To the scorched, blackened woods, where
    the wounded trees
Wait with their old wise patience for the heavenly
    rain,
Sure of the sky: sure of the sea to send its healing
    breeze,
Sure of the sun. And even as to these
Surely the Spring, when God shall please,
Will come again like a divine surprise
To those who sit to-day with their great Dead, hands in
    their hands, eyes in their eyes,
At one with Love, at one with Grief: blind to the
    scattered things and changing skies.

Charlotte Mew

ABOVE: *5 September 1919: British soldiers outside Thiepval*

BELOW: *The Germans adopted a scorched earth policy as they withdrew*

OPPOSITE: *Infantryman on the Somme battlefield in danger from enemy fire*

FOR THE FALLEN

With proud thanksgiving, a mother for her children,
England mourns for her dead across the sea.
Flesh of her flesh they were, spirit of her spirit,
Fallen in the cause of the free.

Solemn the drums thrill: Death august and royal
Sings sorrow up into immortal spheres.
There is music in the midst of desolation
And a glory that shines upon our tears.

They went with songs to the battle, they were young,
Straight of limb, true of eye, steady and aglow.
They were staunch to the end against odds
    uncounted,
They fell with their faces to the foe.

They shall grow not old, as we that are left grow old:
Age shall not weary them, nor the years condemn.
At the going down of the sun and in the morning
We will remember them.

They mingle not with their laughing comrades again;
They sit no more at familiar tables of home;
They have no lot in our labour of the day-time;
They sleep beyond England's foam.

But where our desires are and our hopes profound,
Felt as a well-spring that is hidden from sight,
To the innermost heart of their own land they are
    known
As the stars are known to the Night;

As the stars that shall be bright when we are dust,
Moving in marches upon the heavenly plain,
As the stars that are starry in the time of our
    darkness,
To the end, to the end, they remain.

Laurence Binyon

INDEX OF FIRST LINES

Acknowledgements

The editor and publishers gratefully acknowledge the permission to reproduce copyright material.

Laurence Binyon: *'For The Fallen'* reprinted by permission of The Society of Authors as the Literary Representative of Laurence Binyon.

Vera Brittain: *'To My Brother'* reprinted by permission of the literary executors of Vera Brittain's estate.

Margaret Postgate Cole: *'The Veteran'* and *'The Falling Leaves'* reprinted by permission of David Higham Associates.

e. e. Cummings: *'My Sweet Old Etcetera'* reprinted by permission of W. W. Norton and Faber and Faber.

Eleanor Farjeon: *'Easter Monday'* and *'Now That You Too Must Shortly Go The Way'* reprinted by permission of David Higham Associates.

Gilbert Frankau: *'The Deserter'* from The Faber Book of War Poetry reprinted by permission of AP Watt Ltd on behalf of Timothy d'Arch Smith.

Robert Frost: *'Not To Keep'* from The Poetry of Robert Frost edited by Edward Connery Latham, published by Jonathon Cape, reprinted by permission of The Random House Group Ltd.

Wilfred Gibson: *'The Ridge: 1919'*, *'In The Ambulance'* and *'Breakfast'*, reprinted by permission of Macmillan Publishers Limited.

Robert Graves: *'The Leveller'*, *'A Dead Boche'* and *'The Dead Fox Hunter'* from Collected Poems, reprinted by permission of Carcanet Press Limited.

Ivor Gurney: *'Billet'*, *'Of Grandcourt'*, *'Strange Hells'*, *'The Silent One'* and *'First Time In'* from Ivor Gurney Collected Poems, reprinted by permission of Carcanet Press Limited.

Paul Muldoon: *'Truce'* reprinted by permission of Faber and Faber.

Ezra Pound: *'Poem'* and the extract from *'Hugh Selwyn Mauberley'* from Personae, reprinted by permission of New Directions Publishing Corp. and Faber and Faber.

Edgell Rickword: *'Winter Warfare'* from Collected Poems, reprinted by permission of Carcanet Press Limited.

Siegfried Sassoon: *'Attack'*, *'They'*, *'Remorse'*, *'The General'*, *'The Dug-Out'*, *'The Hero'* and *'To The Warmongers'* reprinted by permission of Barbara Levy Literary Agency and Viking Penguin.

Wallace Stevens: *'The Death Of A Soldier'*, reprinted by permission of Faber and Faber and Alfred Knopf Inc.

W. B. Yeats: *'An Irish Airman Foresees His Death'* from The Collected Poems of W. B. Yeats, reprinted by permission of A. P. Watt on behalf of Gráinne Yeats.